Speculations from Economy

Charles Baron Clarke

Alpha Editions

This edition published in 2024

ISBN : 9789361472275

Design and Setting By
Alpha Editions
www.alphaedis.com
Email - info@alphaedis.com

As per information held with us this book is in Public Domain.
This book is a reproduction of an important historical work. Alpha Editions uses the best technology to reproduce historical work in the same manner it was first published to preserve its original nature. Any marks or number seen are left intentionally to preserve its true form.

Contents

INTRODUCTION ....- 1 -

1. EFFICIENCY OF LABOUR. ....- 2 -

2. RECIPROCITY AND RETALIATION. ....- 7 -

3. UNIVERSAL FREE TRADE. ....- 12 -

4. THE RANSOM OF THE LAND. ....- 17 -

5. MAKING THE MOST OF OUR LAND. ....- 21 -

6. FREE TRADE IN RAILWAYS. ....- 28 -

7. REFORM IN LAND LAW. ....- 35 -

8. EQUALISING OF TAXATION. ....- 38 -

9. WEALTH OF THE NATION. ....- 41 -

INTRODUCTION

The following nine articles are "Speculations," by no means altogether recommendations. They are *from* Political Economy, i.e. they have nearly all of them been suggested by considering mere propositions of Political Economy. Some of them are old, or given me by friends: some are, I believe, new: these many persons will set aside as unpractical or impracticable, as that is the approved word by which people indicate that an idea is new to them. The topics of the nine articles have been largely taken from those now under political discussion, but they can hardly be called ephemeral; and, though they do not form a treatise, they will hardly be called disconnected. As they are speculations, no trouble has been taken to work out suggestions in detail, or give the "shillings and pence" correctly.

1. EFFICIENCY OF LABOUR.

Political economists have not overlooked efficiency of labour: they have underestimated its importance in the opinion of Edward Wilson, who has supplied me with the examples and arguments that follow and who has verbally given me leave to publish as much as I like.

The English workman, especially in a country town of moderate size, regards capital as unlimited, employment ("work") as limited. A wall six feet high is to be built along the length of a certain garden: if one bricklayer is employed, the fewer bricks he lays daily the more days' employment he will get; if several bricklayers are employed, the fewer bricks one lays daily the more employment is left for the others. It thus appears that the more inefficient the labourer is, the better for himself, his fellow-handicraftsmen, and for "labour" in general: the more money is drawn from the capitalist.

There is a grain of truth in this view with respect to petty unavoidable repairs in a narrow locality: but the capital spent on such is as a drop in the ocean compared with that embarked in a single large work. Consider the case of the London Building Trade, as practised in the suburbs on all sides of London. The London bricklayers thoroughly believe that it is their interest to be inefficient: it is said that they have a rule that no bricklayer shall ever lay a brick with the right hand; they have also a rule against "chasing," i.e. that no bricklayer, whatever his skill, shall lay more than a certain number of bricks a day; they believe that if the bricklayer laid a larger number of bricks he would get no more pay for a harder day's work, while the "work" would afford employment to a smaller number of labourers. Look however a little further. The speculative builders round London compete against each other, so that they carry on their trade on ordinary trade profits. Such a builder is building streets, house after house, each house costing him £800, and selling for £1000 say; and this, after paying his interest at the bank, etc., pays him about 10 to 15 per cent on his own capital embarked. Suppose now that the bricklayers increase their inefficiency either by a trade rule or by a combination to shorten the hours of labour. The cost of each house is increased £50 to him: nothing in the new bricklaying rules or rates affects the purchasers; the builder estimates that his profits will fall to 5 to 8 per cent on his capital. He does not care to pursue so risky a business at this rate of profit; he determines to contract operations. When he goes to his bank, a branch of one of the gigantic London joint-stock banks, at the end of the quarter, the manager of the branch comes forward as usual ready to continue the bank advances; but the builder says simply, "The building trade is not so good as it was," and declines. The increased cost of bricklaying has affected all other speculative builders in much the same way; the consequence is that "gold" accumulates in the branch banks. The secretaries and managers of the great joint-stock banks do not let their capital idly accumulate; they buy New Zealand 6 per cents, or transfer to Frankfort or New York the capital that, but for the rise in cost of bricklaying, would have gone to the London bricklayers.

In this case it is easy to see that the quantity of work to be done is not limited. Should the cost of building diminish but a little, the rate of profit of the builders on their *own* capital (in many cases not one-tenth of the capital they employ) will run up to 20 or 30 per cent, or even more; and at even a 20 per cent profit the bricklayers would find that a perfect rage for building would set in. Every speculative builder in the trade would strain his credit to the utmost, and take up every £100 from his bank that he could induce the bank manager to let him have.

A second illustration. Forty years ago, on our farm in the south of England, two men with flails used to begin threshing wheat in the long barn about 1st November, and used to thresh till 1st April. They got eight shillings a week with us, but in adjoining counties seven shillings (and even six) were winter wages. Now the steam threshing-machine will empty that long barn in two short days' work. It takes half a dozen men to do the work, and they get about fifteen shillings a week, though their labour is much shorter and easier than that of the old flail men. At the same time our farmers now are much poorer men than they were forty years ago: they have less capital, they have made for many years past a low rate of profit, and they are frequently themselves complaining that they cannot afford to pay their labourers well, and inferring that they should get Protection back again in some shape or other. The labourers on their part imagine very generally that their increased wages for less work are due to Mr. Arch and agitation; that the employers of labour will never pay more than is wrested from them (this is in large measure true); and that employers must pay whatever agitators are strong enough to demand (this is wholly erroneous).

In this case it is evident on the surface that the labourers who thresh with the steam-thresher are more efficient than the flail-men: their labour is worth the half-a-crown a day to the employer, and therefore the employer, however poor, can afford to pay it as he receives it back with a profit. On the other hand, if the flail-men were raised from the dead, no farmer would now pay them even eight shillings a week for threshing; their labour would not be worth even that.

One illustration more. Thirty years ago there were few more wretched trades than the shoemakers of Northampton. Wages were low, the labour was severe, the social condition of the workmen was necessarily low also.

The sewing-machine, with some special adaptations to make it sew leather, increased about sixfold the bootmaking power of a workman. It is needless to say that the Northampton shoemakers met the introduction of this machine with the fiercest opposition: they said five-sixths of their number must be thrown out of employment. The struggle was won by the machine (as in other cases); shoemakers' wages have ruled 50 to 100 per cent higher ever since, at the same time that the shoemaking population has largely increased; and the social comforts and character of the workpeople have improved vastly too. This is an example that has always puzzled the workmen themselves; but it requires no explanation after what has been said about the efficiency of labour. The puzzle to the shoemakers is what becomes of the additional boots and shoes made. They do not reflect that, even of a necessary of life, only a certain quantity is used at a certain price. Nothing is more necessary in London, especially in winter, than coal; but, when coal some years ago went up to 40s. a ton in London, it was marvellous how people in all ranks managed to reduce their consumption of coal. Much more in the case of boots, which will bear the cost of export to remote countries, did the demand increase as the price fell. A fall of 10 per cent only in the price of boots would cause every wholesale boot exporter to export on the largest scale. No doubt the invention of a self-acting machine which should turn out 1000 pairs of boots an hour at a nominal cost of workmanship per pair would reduce the shoemakers of Northampton to idleness and starvation. But in practice it has rarely happened that any machine has been introduced in any trade that has thus completely choked the increased demand. It has happened often that the workmen who could only work the old way, and were not able to take up the new machine, have been reduced to starvation. Even then, after this generation has passed away, the new machine-workers have been better off than their predecessors.

Employers of labour cannot pay as wages more than the labour is worth: no organisation or rules will make them. But employers may pay a good deal less than the labour is worth, and often have done so. However great their profits, there is, according to J. S. Mill, always a tacit understanding among all employers of labour to pay the minimum the labourers can be induced to accept. It is only by combination that the labourers can get the full value of their efficiency. Here Mr. Arch comes in: I have little doubt that the flail-threshers might, under a well-managed large trade combination, have got nine shillings a week instead of eight shillings forty years ago.

But every rise in wages gained by the workmen, unless springing from or in conjunction with an increase in efficiency, will tell against themselves; it must increase the price of the article, whether houses, wheat, or boots; this must diminish the demand for the article, and this must throw some of the workmen out of employ.

It is difficult to find an example of price of wages which presents any difficulty of explanation when we apply to it the consideration of efficiency. If bricklayers were to offer to exert themselves to the utmost, and do in eight hours the same amount and quality of work they now do in nine, the speculative builders would doubtless be willing to give the same wages for eight hours' work that they now give for nine. In case the labourers by increase in their efficiency are able to get higher wages, the choice will (in general) lie with them how much of the increase they take in increased money wages, how much they take in shortened hours of labour. We thus see how, in an uncivilised community, owing to the inefficiency of their labour, their whole time and energies are expended on their hunting, or otherwise providing bare subsistence. The greater skill of our civilised labourers, working with machines provided by our science, and profiting by our fixed capital (as our railway tunnels and embankments), is vastly more efficient: it ensures the labourers a certainty and regularity of food which the savage does not enjoy, and provides him a certain margin of leisure beyond what the inefficient savage labourer can count upon; it also provides the whole surplus production out of which the intellectual and leisure classes are supported.

It is to be noted that an increase of efficiency in any industry (and very largely in the case of industries producing generally essential utilities) raises real wages in all other industries, and this, whether the particular trade gains (as we have seen it nearly always do) or loses, as is conceivable, though rarely occurring. Thus, if the introduction of a boot-sewing machine lowers the price of boots 50 per cent, this can have no effect in lowering the money wages of farm labourers; and, as a matter of fact, the fall in cost of boots has sensibly improved the position of farm labourers. In the same way the superior efficiency of carriers by railway over the old road carriers has diminished the cost of coal and all articles (the bulky ones most sensibly) in all parts of England. There thus arises the instructive result that handicrafts in which there has been no improvement in the last forty years have obtained a rise of real wages (amounting in some cases to 50 per cent) by the improvements in efficiency in all the trades around them.

To sum up: No man in ordinary business will give a price for anything that he intends to sell again unless he expects to profit by selling it again. No capitalist will pay a workman to make a table unless he expects to sell the table for a sum somewhat exceeding the cost of the wood and the workman's labour. It follows directly that the one grand object of the workman, both as an individual, a trade, and a class, should be to improve the efficiency of his labour. He may gain something by combination and higgling for the turn of the market, but the limit to what he can get is the value of his labour to his employer.

In order to attain this improved efficiency the most important practical aid is piecework. This has done much even in agriculture: the turnip-hoer by the acre earns more, while he does his work at his own time with more comfort to himself than the old day-labourer. What is more important, the men who by head and hand are superior at turnip-hoeing are able to do the work cheaper than ordinary labourers, and turnip-hoeing thus falls entirely to the most efficient hoers, whose efficiency thus again gets constantly improved. There is no doubt to me that, if the London bricklayers would arrange to work by contract, they would soon obtain more wages without being compelled (as they imagine would be the case) to work more severely or longer hours to gain those wages. If they were more efficient, nothing could prevent the competition of employers soon giving extra wages for extra value of work.

But it may, finally, be urged that there is surely such a thing as over-production. If there is an over-production of boots, trade is flat, the wholesale dealers find they are making no profit, they stop their purchases, the workmen are thrown out of employ on a large scale. To this the reply is that there is almost a necessary alternation of up and down in every particular trade, whether the efficiency of the workmen is high or low. If trade is good, the large dealers will extend their purchases, and very commonly rather over-extend their purchases: a reaction follows, and *vice versa* when trade is bad.

But it must be recollected over-production in all trades at once is impossible: capital is now not buried in pots by our great joint-stock banks; if one trade is at standstill the capital is carried to the most remunerative use that the experienced bank secretaries can discover. If agriculture is, as we have lately seen it, in a depressed state for years, inasmuch as wheat is "over-produced" in America till the price in England falls to 36s. per quarter (and less), at which it hardly pays to produce it in England; this of itself implies an enormous spur to all other industries—the real cost of labour has in them fallen (for the labourer will not be able to keep to himself the whole benefit of cheapened food)—the rate of profit in all other industries has risen (*pro tanto*). If we ever do arrive at a state when all the desires are fully satisfied—when there is over-production in all industries—we shall have general reduction in the hours of labour: "efficiency" will take that form.

2. RECIPROCITY AND RETALIATION.

The wealth of England is the sum of the wealth of each individual in England. An individual may have £10,000 in England, £5000 invested in Australia. We may reckon his wealth in England either as including or excluding the £5000, which he could transfer (probably very speedily) to England in gold if he desired it tangibly. Whichever way we reckon his wealth and that of other individuals, we shall in like manner in the sum get the wealth of England: it will be in one case the wealth in England-in the other case the wealth in England plus the lien which residents in England have on other countries in the world.

In parallel manner the effective capital of England, which can be brought into the wages fund, must be the sum of the capital of all the individuals.

These two self-evident truths are capable of many applications: we see directly from them that the National Debt, so far as it is held by residents in England, neither diminishes the national wealth nor affects the wages fund. We see also directly that any exchange between an Englishman and a foreigner which gives a profit to the Englishman gives an equal profit to the English nation.

When a merchant buys 1000 quarters of wheat from America and pays in gold, he does so to make a profit for himself; but he cannot make a profit for himself without making an equal profit for the nation. The exchange of the wheat for gold is profitable to both seller and buyer; otherwise the bargain would not be struck. A value is added to the wheat by its being brought from Minnesota (where it is wanted, as all good things are wanted) to London, where it is much more wanted, and this increased value is greater than the cost of moving the wheat from Minnesota to London; this excess is the profit on the exchange which the buyer and seller divide between them. The exact shares in which they divide the profit between them depend on some of the most complicated considerations in the science of political economy. Indeed, political economy can no more work out a case in figures, even when every circumstance is given, than political economy can tell in pounds sterling what should be the rent of a given farm. But the point required for our present purpose is easy and certain,— unless the English buyer got *some* share in the profit he would not give his gold for the wheat.

The great principle of Free Trade is that in this, and in all similar cases, the individual shall be left to make what profit he can; that his dealings with foreigners shall be interfered with by Government in no way; that he shall not be checked in his operations by import duties, bounties on exports, staples, or any other of the numerous obsolete interferences in the statute-book. The principle is that each individual can manage his own trade better than Government can manage it for him; that, therefore, Government shall let any individual do his best in trade his own way, knowing that whatever profit an individual makes in foreign trade is an equal national profit.

It may be shortly stated that in the old Protectionist theory, destroyed by Adam Smith, gold was considered to be wealth. Hence, if an individual bought foreign wheat for gold, the English suffered a national loss of wealth, and the foreign nation made a national gain. It is unnecessary to occupy space in refuting this (to us absurd) idea, as no refutation can be more satisfactory than Adam Smith's own.

If I profit on the transaction of buying 1000 quarters of wheat for gold, I do so irrespectively of all other exchanges by others. Whether the firm next door to me has succeeded in selling to a Boston house £2000 worth of Sheffield cutlery or no is a matter entirely beside my bargain. My profit will depend practically on the movements in the English corn trade: a small rise in the price of wheat at Mark Lane between the date of my purchasing by cable the wheat in America and my selling it at Mark Lane, may give me a large profit, or *vice versa*. But my exchange of gold for the wheat is a separate transaction of itself: it stands entirely on its own bottom.

It is perfectly true that if my neighbour in Threadneedle Street does succeed in selling £2000 worth of cutlery to the New Englander, there is another distinct national profit to England and to America. [Footnote: I am assuming for simplicity throughout that every exchange made by private merchants in this foreign trade is a successful speculation; if in any particular speculation a merchant loses, his country loses the same amount. As foreign trade, on the whole, is an enormous national profit, I am justified in sinking the particular cases of loss. It may be said, "But perhaps all your exchange of gold for wheat is a national loss": it is evident that when the trade takes this form the merchants who import foreign corn stop their operations instantly; in practice they stop them with prescient instinct.] But whether he succeeds in making a bargain or not, I object to being interfered with by Government, and prevented making my own little profit. If my neighbour is practically deprived of his profitable bargain by Government action on the part of the Americans—if they are Protectionists and believe that gold is the only National Wealth, and put a heavy duty on cutlery—if by doing this they prevent an exchange profitable to both nations—they stop TWO merchants from a profitable stroke of business. Whether they injure the English merchant or the Bostonian would-be purchaser of cutlery MOST is (as above explained) very difficult to prove in any well-ascertained instance, but it is quite certain that the interference of the American import duty causes a loss to each merchant and to each nation.

Where now is Reciprocity and where Retaliation? We can no doubt say to the Americans, "As you have injured us in the matter of cutlery, so will we injure you by putting a duty on wheat." But it is merely cutting off one's nose to spite one's face. In the exchange of gold for wheat the division of the profit on one transaction is uncertain, but in the long run it is probably about equal between the English and the American merchants, i.e. between the English and the American nations. (I am not overlooking the fact that the ultimate benefit to England is cheap bread; but it is unnecessary in the present argument to follow the food down the throats of the consumers: the wheat is really worth to the corn merchants what they can get for it from the consumers.) We cannot stop the corn trade with America by a duty (or diminish it) without as great a loss to ourselves (probably a greater) than to them; the retaliation in putting a duty on corn because the Americans put a duty on cutlery would be (with our lights) mere spite: it would be as though a farmer who took one sample of wheat to market and one of barley, should meet a factor who offered him his price for the wheat, but would not spring to his price for the barley, and the farmer should thereupon sulkily carry both his samples home again.

The ideas of Reciprocity and Retaliation are pure relics of the old Protectionist commercial theory, viz. that there is always a national loss in parting with gold—that the foreign trade can only be profitable to England so long as the value of the exports exceeds that of the imports, so that a continual accumulation of gold may go on.

Now, first, we may meet this with the abstract scientific argument that there is no character by which gold can be diagnosed as wealth from steel or broadcloth. Our merchant who buys wheat for gold could buy from the Americans wheat for cutlery or wheat for broadcloth. The reason he gives gold for the wheat is merely because he makes a better profit by giving gold than by giving anything else in exchange for the wheat. The nation therefore gets a better profit that way too.

Descending a little from this abstract argument, our opponent says, "If you go on buying wheat for gold, and cannot sell your cutlery and broadcloth out of the country for gold, you *must* run out of gold." But the fact has been proved by many years' experience not so to be: for many years our imports have been some £150,000,000 sterling more than our exports, while our stock of gold in the Bank of England (and the gold in circulation) remain the same from year to year. This is one of those many things (like the supply of meat to London) which will regulate itself perfectly and insensibly (without any violent disturbances in trade or the money market) if Government will only leave the matter entirely alone. If our stock of gold is at all short our merchants give a little less per quarter for American wheat; the trade is checked; the sensibility of the market—the experience of our corn-traders—is such that the balance is preserved with very slight oscillations. The refusal of the Americans (enforced by an import duty) to purchase our cutlery, etc., *does* partially check the reflux of gold to this country, and does lower sensibly the price which the Americans get for their wheat from us. Errors in political economy avenge themselves—often fearfully—on their perpetrators. But our objector will still want to have explained to him where the £150,000,000 sterling required in England annually comes from. It is not essential to, or indeed any part of, my present argument to explain this; but I will anticipate matters so far as to say shortly here that this £150,000,000 is, roughly speaking, the interest on English capital invested in foreign countries paid in cash to the owners resident in England—it is equivalent to an annual tribute.

Professor Henry Fawcett's *Lectures on Free Trade* is a sound and admirable book: it is occupied a good deal with the practical question why so few foreign nations have adopted Free Trade, and how such foreign nations are to be converted to the orthodox creed of Adam Smith. But, as I think, unfortunately Professor Fawcett has in that book used the words Reciprocity and Retaliation pretty freely. Their mere use is enough to fortify a French or American Protectionist in his present policy; he naturally says, "The English Free-traders themselves admit that we are making money out of them: we take their gold for our wine and wheat; we refuse to give our gold for their cutlery and broadcloth: those English have now to come to us whining for Reciprocity; as to their Retaliation we are not alarmed—we know they *must* have wheat and *will* have wine." I would wish to expunge the words Reciprocity and Retaliation from the subject, as being words merely suggestive of false views. But the most fatal course to the adoption of a Free Trade policy by foreign nations has been our plan of humbling, begging (and indirectly giving a consideration for) Commercial Treaties. Such a course is enough to (and does) counterbalance with foreign nations all our theoretical writings about Free Trade. We go to France and say, "We will let in your wines at a lower duty provided you do us the favour and give us the advantage of lowering your duties on English manufactures." I cannot conceive any way of putting the matter more strongly calculated to convince the French that we believe we lose by purchasing their wines and gain by selling them our manufactures.

It appears to me that if we wish to convince Europe and America of the truth of Free Trade (as understood by our political economists), our proper course is to adopt Free Trade ourselves FULLY (if the principle is good for wheat it is good for tea—I shall return to this), and then to say to foreigners, "See how we prosper under Free Trade." If the Americans continue to maintain Protectionist duties on our manufactures, our line of conduct is not to offer to pay them indirectly to relax those duties, but to say, "You are losing more by your duties than we are; the proof of the pudding is in the eating." If I believe, as I do, that the Americans are gaining less wealth under Protection than they would under Free Trade, I cannot imagine any plan less likely to convert them to my views than my going to them and saying, "We will give you £5,000,000 sterling (or some valued political advantage) if you will alter your mistaken policy." If this course did not confirm the Americans in the very deepest suspicions that Protection is really advantageous to them, and that we in our inmost heart think so too, my ideas of human nature are altogether at fault. But every foreign debate, whether in France, Germany, or America, on Free Trade, convinces me that I am not mistaken in the effect which I attribute to our prayers to every foreign nation to grant us a Commercial Treaty.

3. UNIVERSAL FREE TRADE.

Wheat is now admitted to England free of duty. Tea pays a duty of about £4,000,000 sterling a year. This is called a duty for revenue, not for protection. Tea is an article of universal consumption; the tax on it is open to the objections against a poll tax or hearth tax, viz. that by it many a poor old woman is taxed as heavily as far richer people; indeed, owing to the poor consuming the lower-priced teas, they are by the present duty taxed at a higher rate than those who can afford the more expensive teas.

The reply in defence of these anomalies is, "We have to raise £4,000,000 sterling by a duty on something; on whatever we put it, it will no doubt be bad." Granting, however, this for a moment, the onus lies on the defender of the existing tariff to prove that it is better to raise the £4,000,000 required from tea than from wheat, or than to raise £2,000,000 from tea, £2,000,000 from wheat. Mr. Raban, a leading tea-planter in Assam, has observed that if the duty on tea was replaced by one on wheat to raise the same gross amount, the pressure on the English poor would be less; while an encouragement would thus be given both to tea-planting in India and to agriculture in England. I adduce this case of the duty on tea merely to bring out strongly the fact that Free Trade in wheat is not universal Free Trade. I do not recommend that the duty on tea should be replaced by other duties: I am going to raise the question whether it should not be replaced by direct taxation.

In the case of tea, the duty can hardly be said to be "protective," except so far as by raising the cost of tea it impels English drinkers to have more free recourse than they otherwise would to other drinks; but in a large number of cases a duty operates both as a revenue and as a protective duty. It is a curious fact that the farmers, after unanimously struggling FOR the duty on wheat because it was a protective duty, subsequently unanimously struggled for thirty years AGAINST the malt tax (involving a duty on barley) because it was a revenue duty. As soon, however, as the malt duty was repealed, they discovered that it had been a protective duty; barley fell in price (malting samples) about 12s. a quarter, and has never recovered, nor does any farmer now suppose it ever will. This is rather a complex case, because on the abolition of the malt tax an equal tax (in gross amount) was put on beer; and it might be supposed at first sight that this would not affect the price of barley. It has in several ways: Firstly, Many brewers now brew common beer with one-third malt, two-thirds molasses, cane sugar, etc. The tax being on the beer, Government no longer cares whether it is brewed from malt or from rubbish, and the consumers grow soon accustomed to the lowered taste of malt in their beer; Secondly, The admission of foreign malt and barley without duty has quickened the importation by removing those restraints and interferences which hamper trade out of all proportion to their expressed amounts in pounds, shillings, and pence.

In order to establish a Universal Free Trade and to make every port in England a free port, it would be necessary to raise by direct taxation about £40,000,000 annually, because the excise on beer, etc., would have to be abandoned with the Customs duties. We will consider the possibility of raising this £40,000,000 by direct taxation before we dilate on the advantages which would follow Universal Free Trade.

Ricardo, at the end of his masterly consideration of the effect of taxation variously levied, comes to the general conclusion that the best tax is that which is least in amount. Adam Smith and the older economists held that one test which a well-devised tax had to satisfy was that it should take the money from the taxpayer insensibly, indirectly. Now, all taxes that thus insensibly drain the taxpayers invariably take more in gross from them than reaches the Government. To raise £40,000,000 by customs and excise costs about £3,000,000; so that the people have to pay £43,000,000, while the Government gets £40,000,000. In direct taxes, as income taxes, property rates, the cost of collection is very small—about two-pence in the pound. In public as in private business it is much more economic to look payments in the face and make them with our eyes open than to let the money slip away in driblets. Moreover, modern politicians think, in opposition to Adam Smith, that it has a good moral effect on the body politic to be made to feel exactly what taxes they pay, so that they cannot help knowing whenever taxation is increased.

A serious objection to indirect taxation is that it always falls with unfair weight on the poor, as in the case of tea duties stated above. It may be urged that the existing duties are (except tea) nearly all on luxuries, as beer, spirits, tobacco. But the English have drunk beer for many hundred years; the taste for beer is largely fixed by inheritance; beer as supplying sustenance in a form that *rapidly* assists exhausted nature is, to very many at least, as much a necessary of life as tea is. Whether we believe tobacco to be injurious or not, we have no right to impose on an article so very largely consumed a duty which amounts to taxing the poor out of proportion to the rich.

If all the indirect taxes are removed, the poor (at least down to those earning £1 a week and upwards) must be made to contribute to direct taxes. It may be urged against Universal Free Trade that the poor are so ignorant that they would sooner pay sixteen-pence a week in taxes indirectly than eightpence directly. This might prove a fatal objection to carrying out Universal Free Trade at the first attempt; but one of the objects to be gained by direct taxation is the education of the people. It may also be urged that the whole political power being now in the hands of the masses, they are so selfish and unjust that if taxation is made a plain matter they will put all taxation on the rich and refuse to pay anything themselves. The reply to this is, If this is your estimate of the understanding and morality of the masses, you should not have put the whole political power in their hands.

We are only attempting at present to show that the £40,000,000 sterling (to replace duties and those parts of the excise which hang on duties) *could* be raised by direct taxation: we are not attempting to show the best way it could be raised by direct taxation; it will be seen hereafter that a portion of it might perhaps be better raised by a National Property Rate.

The £40,000,000 would be raised by an income tax of sixteen-pence in the pound—(I am underestimating safely—about a shilling in the pound would raise it really),—carried down to £156 a year without any reductions; while incomes of £1 a week paid eightpence weekly, and incomes of £2 a week paid twelvepence weekly. In the Crimean War the nation endured an income tax of sixteen-pence in the pound; it is certain that the nation is richer now, and better able to bear such a rate.

But this is not the strength of the argument. In the Crimean War England endured sixteen-pence in the pound *extra*, in addition to all existing taxes (some of which were raised too), and the capital thus taken from the people was destroyed (much of it) or dissipated in the Crimea. But the sixteen-pence in the pound here suggested would be in lieu of an equal amount of taxes taken off (it would be rather less in amount than the taxes taken off): the nation therefore, would not feel it at all, though individuals would feel it in different ways. A poor man would have eightpence a week deducted from his wages, but he would get his beer at three-fifths the present price, his tea at two-thirds the present price, etc. He would soon feel that he gained by the change. The rich would find that they lost; but that loss would, I believe, be made up to them over and over again.

First, I believe it is impossible to realise the effect on our trade of having London, Liverpool, etc., free ports. We possess at present half the ocean trade of the world: with our ports free, we should get a yet larger share of the world's trade, and secure it permanently. That is to say, we should certainly keep it until other nations adopted Universal Free Trade.

Secondly, The fall in the price of tea, beer, etc., would be more than the amount of the tax remitted: the freedom of universal manufacture without any Government interference, the liberty to land tea without delay, and put it into the market without having to advance the duty, would cause at once a great activity in the trades, and at the same time a fall in price. By diminishing the need for middle-men the quality of the beer, tea, etc., would be raised, and adulteration diminished.

Thirdly, The fall in the price of tea and beer would bring down the price of all competing drinks: it would at first diminish the consumption of competing drinks. The cheapening the price of some of the prime necessaries of life would be to some extent divided between capital and labour. As in the case of wheat, the labourer would be made better off, while the profits of capital would be raised. A general and permanent improvement in all trades would result, except possibly in those of the tea-dealer and brewer—but I do not think they would lose. I see no end to the developments from Universal Free Trade: we can only gain some idea of what they would be by tracing as far as we may what the results of Free Trade in one article—wheat—have been; and in doing this we must recollect that before 1846 the quantity of wheat imported was trifling compared with the present importation.

To this scheme of direct taxation Edward Wilson objects, "Taxation should fall on expenditure, not on income." It is true that our object must always be to encourage accumulation, and discourage destruction of capital (expenditure). Practically, it does not appear that a heavy income tax diminishes the taste for accumulation in England: it does increase the tendency of large capitalists to invest their capital out of England, so as to avoid the State charges on capital in England. But the capital in England and the quantity of English capital invested abroad are already so enormous that the "tendency" of an increased income tax may be disregarded. Lastly, it may be objected, Would the sixteen-pence income tax levied as you propose (or nearly so) raise £40,000,000? At the time of the Crimean War each penny in the pound income tax brought in a million sterling. At the present time, each penny in the pound income tax brings in nearer two millions sterling, but the productiveness of the tax is much interfered with by the large remissions now allowed, and subtractions which take effect just where the contributors to the tax are most numerous, say from £100 to £300 a year. I therefore reckon that, without remissions, the tax of sixteen-pence in the pound down to £156 a year would produce about £30,000,000, and that the tax down to £52 a year would about produce the rest. The *total* income that income tax is now levied on is nearly £600,000,000. We need not be surprised at the productiveness of the income tax. A man of £10,000 a year pays tax on that. But he has a steward on £300 a year, he is worth to his firm of lawyers £100 a year, and so on: these pay income tax on the £300 and the £100 over again. When the income tax is carried down to incomes on £1 a week, the tax will be levied on the same income over and over again. Even a spendthrift with £10,000 a year usually scatters more than he actually destroys.

Lastly, It has not been overlooked that there is an income tax now: and if the whole proceeds of the sixteen-pence income tax were used to fill up the deficiency in customs and excise, then we have to make up a deficiency equal to the present proceeds of the income tax. This might be done (to start with) by the National Property Rate now to be suggested. But the expectation is, that with Universal Free Trade, and the tremendous stimulus thereby given to commerce and manufacture, the National Income would rise with a bound, and that in two or three years a much lower rate than sixteen-pence income tax in the pound would supply the amount of all the indirect taxes abandoned.

4. THE RANSOM OF THE LAND.

Many people see quite clearly that, the population of England being 25,000,000, the next baby born has a right to one twenty-fifth-millionth part of the area of England in soil of average fertility. The arrangements of society by which the laud is partitioned among a limited class, and the complicated rights sanctioned by law in one plot of land, are considered of no validity as against the natural right of the new-born baby. I do not see this theory to be self-evident: on the other hand the supporters of it always give it as fundamental, axiomatic; they no doubt presume rightly that the land is limited, and that if one man holds more than his arithmetical share, he must push out somebody else from his arithmetical share: while a man who keeps a hundred pocket-knives does not perceptibly hinder other people having numerous pocket-knives. Still I do not see how this consideration weighs against Lord Derby's title to his lands, if the body politic has determined that on the whole it is best for the community that land should not be held equally by all, and sanctions by law Lord Derby's monopoly of a large area. On the theory of the natural right of every infant born to its arithmetical share, the monopolisers of land are liable to a perpetually recurring ransom: this can only practically be carried out by a special National Rate on Real Property (*i.e.* Land, with the houses, mines, etc., inseparably attached to it), which must be in addition to such taxes as income tax, succession duty, etc., which land already suffers equally with trades, professions, offices, and personalty. The local rates in England exceed £25,000,000 annually; and the ratepayers perhaps reckon this a large enough ransom. I should remark in passing that one man with 1000 acres of land does not dispossess any more babies of their rights than do ten men with 100 acres each. The ransom therefore must be a strictly level rate: to put a higher rate on large holders, or to despoil large holders of a portion of their landed property, will be to work the ransom unfairly. It hence will follow that any heavy ransom is now impracticable. Of late years some farms have gone out of cultivation because they will not pay the tithe, land tax, and rates already on them: to put any heavy ransom on the land would at once throw large areas in England out of cultivation.

The question of the ransom, therefore, is not so all-important as has been considered; the rates at present being £25,000,000, it might be possible to levy an additional national rate of £5,000,000 to keep down the perpetually upspringing rights of new-born infants, without throwing land out of cultivation to any sensible extent. The whole question will lie thus between a total rate of £25,000,000 and £30,000,000. I am about, however, as a corollary to this subject, to suggest a way of forming a National Rate Book which probably would not materially alter the present rating, but which would alter entirely the taking of land for public purposes, and would effectuate all that is good in the phrase the Nationalisation of Land.

This phrase is liberally used but rarely defined. Different orators appear to have quite different ideas as to what it means; and when they explain what they suppose it to mean, they generally prove that, in the way they understand it, it would be serious national damage.

It is unnecessary to observe that landlords now (omitting individual exceptions and idiosyncrasies) expend their best endeavours in getting the best rent they can for their land. They have no prejudices in favour of farms of a particular size; a landlord of a farm of 1000 acres would let it directly in five-acre plots if he could get a better (and equally certain) gross rent by so doing. "Nationalisation" is often taken to mean that Government is to buy land and let it out in small plots. But apart from expense of Government management and objections to Government interference, we may safely assume that there would be a national loss by this procedure: the private owner would discover very quickly if he could make a profit by letting his farms piecemeal.

All Government interference can do to improve the produce of the land is to abolish all restrictive laws, and to make the general tenure of land such that every piece of land shall fall into the hands of that man who is able to make the most of it. The National Rate Book now suggested is designed to accomplish this end. We will subsequently consider how it might assist public companies. As the suggested way of getting a National Rate Book is at first sight rather startling, I would premise that it is no rash invention of mine; it worked admirably in Attica—as see Demosthenes or Boeckh.

To make the National Rate Book, each landowner values (with the magistrate) his land at what price he pleases; the State has the right to buy the land at any time at that price, plus 33-1/3 per cent for compulsory purchase. The magistrate sees that each separate house, farm, and plot is valued separately. No person need prove his title; any man can value any piece of land, and need not prove himself to be owner, tenant, or agent; but any piece of land valued by no one would be claimed as public property.

A man who valued himself unfairly low would not be bought out at once and dispossessed by Government, unless it happened that during that year his land was taken up by Government or by a railway company for some public purpose. The regular course of business would be as follows:—An owner A would put his house and curtilage in the Rate Book at £1200. The sycophant B would come to the magistrate, offer £1600 for the property, and lodge the £1600 with the magistrate. The magistrate then, without divulging the name of the sycophant, would write to A either to rate his house at £1600 (paying a fine for so doing), or to take £1600 for it. If he took the £1600, B would get the property, and Government the increased rate. If A preferred raising his rateable value to £1600, B would get the fine, Government would get the increased rate.

The utmost pressure put upon any owner under this system would be that, if he would not pay rates on x pounds for his property, he would be obliged to take x pounds for the property.

The 33-1/3 per cent for compulsory purchase is illusory, and I have only put it in the statement of the scheme to meet an objection which I know to be common (and equally illusory). It is clear that if I know I am going to get 33-1/3 per cent for compulsory purchase, whether from Government or a secret sycophant, I shall proportionately undervalue my property. Thus if I estimate the real value of my house and curtilage at £1200, and feel that I do not care if I sell at that price, I shall put it down in the Rate Book at £900. This applies to all owners, so that the allowance for compulsory sale would only artificially depreciate by one-fourth all the rateable values put down in the magistrate's book.

I have not stopped to cumber the statement of this simple plan by adding the details necessary to meet severance of a farm by a railway company, etc. The provisions to meet complicated tenures, etc., would run much the same as in the Lands Clauses Consolidation Act.

It will be at once seen that this form of Rate Book would really nationalise the land by bringing each piece into the hands of him who could make most out of it. If I saw my way to use a piece of laud so that it should be worth £1000 to me, and if on looking into the Rate Book I saw that the present owner only considered it worth £600 to him, I should at once lodge my £900 with the magistrate. A few owners would really feel as Naboth. They could indulge this feeling by putting a very high rateable value on their property. The high rates they would thus have to pay would be the due ransom of the land; but in general every piece of land would pass into the hands of him who could make most of it. There would spring up, as in Attica, a large class of professional sycophants. By their incessant operations, properties small and great would be continually passing from the slothful and the old-fashioned to the enterprising and modern-educated. No nationalisation of the land could get so much out of it or conduce so highly to progress as the National Rate Book. We should have companies and adventurers buying up all sorts of pieces of land, just as formerly they speculated in taking up land for mining in Cornwall. We should see an extraordinary activity in the employment of capital in England.

For all public improvements, as a new street or a Government military station, a few minutes with the map and Rate Book would show the Government officer or engineer the best route or plot to take, and would also show him the exact cost of the land for the scheme. There would be no law expenses, no prolonged fights, no juries, no arbitrations.

Wastes, downs, heaths, bogs, would be rated very low. It would be in the power of Government to take up largely and at small cost large areas of Surrey heaths, etc., to provide air and recreation ground for an evergrowing metropolis. In this manner, too, public commons and quasi-public commons might be secured to the public all over England: a public-spirited town-council or a local Kyrle Society would have a wide field and an immense stimulus for action.

I have not stopped to rebut the common (but mistaken) idea that burdens on the land (being in gross not more than the rackrent) affect the cultivation. Partners have long drunk at market dinners "Confusion to the black slug that devours the English farmer." How is it that these farmers did not (do not) see that there are tithe-free farms (and some tithe-free parishes) in England, and that the tenants of such farms get no advantage by being tithe-free?

As I explain elsewhere, a tenant with several years of his lease to run is (economically considered) a part landowner: if the tithe were suddenly abolished, tenants with leases would get relief as well as their landlords. So if a new tax or rate is laid on land (and made payable by the tenant), all tenants with leases will have to pay such tax or rate out of their own pocket so long as their lease lasts; afterwards it will fall wholly on the landlords.

It is repeated now, in nearly every country newspaper, that the English farmer cannot compete with the American grower because of the burdens on the land of England. I will not write out (I cannot improve) Ricardo's proof that rent does not enter into price. The "burdens" on land are really first charges on the rackrent and do not affect a year-to-year tenant at all. When a farmer meditates taking a farm he asks not merely what is the rent: he inquires what is the tithe, what the average amount of the rates (and is that likely to increase or diminish during the next seven years); the intending tenant only wants to know what sum in all he will have to pay for the farm; whether any of this payment is called tithe or not, or whether some of it is quit-rent, or whether he is to pay the land tax for his landlord's convenience,—about all this he cares nothing; they are mere questions of names to him.

5. MAKING THE MOST OF OUR LAND.

John S. Mill, following W. T. Thornton, advocated a system of petty proprietors against the English system of large farms with hired labourers. Figures were quoted to show the splendid produce got by petty proprietors in France and elsewhere—as the result, however, of infinite toil. The petty proprietors were, moreover, shown to be much better off than our hired labourers; and the magic of property combined with independence was represented as having produced a superior class. These things may have been so, at least in some cases and particular countries, at the date (before 1846) when J. S. Mill originally put forward these views. The liberal, and radical writers on political economy and sociology still follow (most of them) on the same side, which has become in a manner historically the liberal side. There is much against it.

First, Production on the large scale is cheaper than on the small; this is as true of agriculture as of other industries. The large farmer has one fixed and one movable steam-engine of his own; he has his own drills, threshing and winnowing machines, reaping and mowing machines. The petty proprietor may hire these, but at a dear rate, and few of them can work to any advantage on his small patches of corn. The large farmer has large fields; he saves area as against the petty proprietors; he has fewer headlands and fences, harbouring weeds and stopping the sun and air. The large farmer can work corn and sheep together; one shepherd and his boy will look after 500 ewes. You may travel 200 miles by rail in France and not see two flocks of sheep. Sheep-farming is seen all the world over to be an industry that pays on the large scale; and the want of it injures the corn produce of the French petty proprietor. Louis Napoleon sent Lavergne to make a report on English farming; the substance of his report is, that were France farmed on the English system by English farmers, the corn produce would be four or five times what it is now; leaving sheep out of the question.

The advocates of peasant-proprietorship, at least the better informed ones, do not now suppose that a peasant receiving a few acres out of a large English average farm (and capital to make a start) could make a subsistence out of it. They believe that peasant-proprietors could maintain themselves on small plots of rich land in and close to towns, working as market-gardeners or cowkeepers rather than as farmers.

This narrows down the peasant-proprietor theory vastly in its practical application; it remains hardly a national question. But I have been astonished to see in the neighbourhood of London of late years the large "gentleman" market-gardeners steadily displacing the smaller and all the single-handed men. The subject is so important that I will take one of two instances in detail. I have seen a gentleman market-gardener, eight miles or so from Covent Garden, growing strawberries, several acres in each patch. He had young men (a separate staff) out at daybreak to keep the birds off. The small gardener, growing a few long beds of strawberries, is ruined by the birds, whether he lets them eat or goes into the expense and labour of netting. The gentleman has his own large spring-vans waiting; these vans are fitted for fruit, and as the pickers gather the strawberries they deliver them in small and frequent parcels to the packers. The moment the first van is laden it starts at three miles per hour and travels to Covent Garden itself, where the strawberries are delivered to the fruit-dealer, who buys them wholesale of the gentleman-gardener. The small grower has to get his strawberries to the local railway station, and to arrange to get them from the London terminus to market; his trouble and expense are considerable; but, more important still, his strawberries do not come into the hands of the wholesale dealer in the "condition" that the large grower's do. This large grower admitted that he was paying £12 an acre per annum for some of his land; he added, "My labour per acre, and even my manure per acre, costs so much that I do not think about a few pounds rent more or less." These gentleman-gardeners are on the average better educated than the small market-gardeners; they travel about the country, gather hints, and pick up new good varieties of strawberries, etc. From their scale of operations and varied sorts of strawberries they can, even in rough wet weather or in drought, always supply to their wholesale dealer some fruit. In fine, they beat the small grower at every point; they undersell him at Covent Garden; they outbid him for desirable garden-land within reach of London. It may be said that in growing plain vegetables the small gardener would not be at such a disadvantage. I will reply (without detailing all my observations) that I have seen the same gentleman-gardener growing a two-acre plot of early radishes, and that he completely spoilt early radishes for all the small gardeners.

The advocates of peasant-proprietors have thought cowkeeping hopeful for small men. In my experience dairies of fifty or sixty cows have an enormous advantage; they can have perfectly designed dairies; they have enough cream to make butter daily throughout the year (which saves much trouble, loss, and occasionally inferior butter); they can maintain approximately a uniform supply. In short, they beat, undersell, and displace the small cowkeepers wherever the large dairy is moderately well managed.

The cottager or peasant-proprietor has, I believe, an advantage in poultry of all kinds. When poultry are kept in very large numbers they are more liable to disease, and the diseases are more disastrous—sweeping off the whole large stock. Fowl and egg farming is one of the most successful, perhaps the most successful point with the French peasant-proprietors. To make birdfarming successful the proper plan is to keep a moderate number of as many birds as possible—fowls, "galeenies," ducks, geese, turkeys, large pigeons—and to go in for eggs as well as fowls. I have not seen peasant-proprietors in England attempting this, which seems to me one of the most hopeful of experiments for them.

The second point urged by Mill, and still by some, is that peasant-proprietors are better off than English labourers. With the present price of agricultural labour in England this seems to be very generally not the case; the French peasant-proprietors and the agricultural lower classes in Germany are (with small exceptions) now worse off than the English farm-labourer; they work very much harder and they get less to eat. The economic truth doubtless is that the hired labourer may or may not be better off than the peasant-proprietor, according to circumstances; and circumstances in England just now are in favour of the hired labourer.

Then as to independence, it may fairly be questioned whether a good agricultural workman, now practically liberated from the Law of Settlement, and who can command a fair wage anywhere, is not really more independent than a French peasant absolutely tied to a three-acre plot for life.

The real difference between the advocates of the nationalisation of the land and the Conservatives is this. The Conservative says, "Leave everything to its natural course, and let us have no Government interference. If the peasant-proprietor really can maintain himself while paying as high a rent as the ordinary farmer, we shall soon have plenty of them." Or, the Conservative has no objection to a philanthropist starting a few picked peasant-proprietors as an experiment. But he objects to starting any gigantic new scheme of working the land, except as a matter of business; he objects to Government philanthropy, which means giving away other people's money.

Our farm-labourers, as a rule, know nothing of gardening, and few of them can command £10 capital. I have sometimes looked round to select a picked man, and wondered whether, if I put him in a selected five-acre plot near a town, and also lent him the £200 or so capital requisite to give him a chance, this picked agricultural labourer would succeed; and I have inclined to think he would not succeed. I need not therefore express any opinion as to what would happen if Government were to take 10,000 or 100,000 farm-labourers, advance them £200 each, and place them in five-acre or ten-acre plots: there would be a tremendous bill to pay, and the plan of peasant-proprietors would be put aside for many a day. If the plan is to be successful it must be introduced gradually and in a business manner, *i.e.* what does not pay must not be persisted in.

The plan, now frequently put forward, that Government is to employ all men out of work to reclaim and bring into cultivation waste lands, is liable to additional objections. Who is to fix the wages, the hours of labour, and the tale of work for the Government labourers? If these were fixed as the advocates of the plan wish them fixed, Government would soon have all the labourers of the country in its employ. If, on the other hand, these were fixed below the market rate, Government would only have such labour as the Poor-Law Unions now have, and which they find hardly worth employing.

Leaving this (practically grave) difficulty aside, if a heath or a moor is now uncultivated it is because nobody sees how it can be profitably brought into cultivation; it can always at a sufficient outlay be reclaimed, but that will not be done unless it is calculated that the rent of the land when reclaimed will pay the interest on the whole expense of reclamation, and something besides. If Government reclaims land that private persons cannot reclaim with profit, we may be sure that Government will suffer a considerable loss. This must be provided out of taxes: are the promoters of reclamation of wastes by Government prepared for this?

The wastes of England are the only land left the public. Elsewhere the public can only walk along a pavement or a high road. The good land is all pretty well in cultivation; and the best of what is left can give but a moderate profit on reclamation, while its enclosure, under Act of Parliament, deprives the public of it for ever. Hence Professor H. Fawcett, throughout his parliamentary career, put his veto with great success on all enclosure schemes. It is possible that there might be a profit on the enclosure of Epping Forest: who will now support that reclamation?

It is very desirable that wealthy private philanthropic individuals and wealthy private philosophic societies, should try experiments in small farming, market-gardening, co-operative farming, reclamation of wastes, etc. There is no hindrance to their so doing: they can readily hire as many farms as they please at cheap rents, and subdivide them, and put in picked labourers with an advance of capital. But that Government should embark in uncertain speculations of this kind is quite another thing.

The safe general principle, whether in the sale of horses, the letting of houses, or the letting of land, is that Government should not interfere; or, to speak more correctly, Government interference should only interfere to prevent restrictive covenants and to ensure Free Trade, so that every article (land included) may pass without restraint into the hands of the man to whom it is worth most. The greater the individual profit the greater the national profit. Under a section headed "Law," below, I will say something about the removal of entail, etc.—a dry but important branch of the question. The National Property Rate, with the aid of sycophants, would remove many obstructions.

There has been much controversy and several Parliamentary Acts concerning the regulation of bargains between landlord and tenant. How a tenant or a landlord can be injured in such a bargain is impossible to understand, except in so far as a man is injured who gives £30 for a horse worth only £20. Will Parliament interfere to protect such horse-purchasers? The matter has been obscured by omitting to notice that a tenant with a long lease at a fixed rent possesses a share (often the larger share) of the "landlord interest," in the language of political economy. As a simple example: A tenant took, say in 1850, a Scotch farm on a Scotch lease absolute of nineteen years, at £500 a year. Within two or three years of his so taking it the rise in wool, potatoes, and other things, caused the value of the farm to rise to £600 a year, and this increased value lasted the whole of his lease and some time after. Now, treating the increase of value of £100 a year as permanent (as it was very soon regarded both by landlord and tenant), it is clear that this £100 a year for the period of the lease (say seventeen years to run) went to the tenant, not to the landlord; and the first seventeen years of an annuity in fee is worth more than all the rest.

It is evident that on a seven years' (absolute) lease the tenant would similarly get a good share (not the larger share) in all the improvement in value that occurred during his lease. Up to ten or twelve years ago the value of land had been rising very steadily in the South of England for near half a century. Rents were pushed up very generally at the termination of every lease, though noblemen, great county gentlemen, the Church, and the Universities, as a rule, never raised the rent on an old tenant; but they could raise the rent all the more by a jump when a new man came in. During all these years the tenant-farmers complained rarely of their leases, though they were often subject to covenant nuisances about cropping, selling off the farm, game, and incoming for the new tenant.

But during the last ten years the process is reversed. A farmer took a farm for £500 a year for seven years in the south of England, and before the lease had run half out the farm was not worth £400 (and in many cases not £300). Here the tenant suffered a heavy loss. When in former years he got a gain he never proposed to allow his landlord 15 per cent extra rent. But now that the drop in value of such farms has taken place, and probably will not proceed further, a tenant who takes a new lease requires no Act of Parliament to protect him: he can protect himself. By the date the Abolition of the Game Laws (a wrong but intelligible phrase) was carried, the farmers in the South of England were in a position not to take any benefit under that Act, but to covenant for all the game and sporting on their farms for themselves. So as to the Act regulating the leases between tenant and landlord, where they chose to avail themselves of it, the tenant now can generally get more favourable terms outside the provisions of the Act. Farms are so down, tenants so scarce, that landlords have to give way on all minor points. Wherever Government interference operates at all, it is almost sure to operate harmfully. Consider for a moment the case of "incoming." Formerly, by the "custom of the country" south of London, the incoming tenant paid for two years' dressing for the corn crops, north of London he paid the outgoing tenant only for one year's dressing, by the custom of the country too. The question practically only amounted to increasing by 5 per cent the capital necessary to take the farm south of London. Now what can be gained by Government interference in such a matter as this, in which each farmer and land-agent was in general in favour of the "custom" he had grown up under?

A prevalent idea is that the land is not highly farmed enough, and that the land of England might be made to yield much more, and that Government is to cause this to be done. It is most unfortunate to raise this theory at the moment when land is "down," i.e. when produce is cheap, labour expensive. Every farmer knows that the only way to meet these conditions is to farm "lower." In a south country farm the farmer will sow much less corn, and try to keep more sheep. In the Western States of America, where produce is very cheap, labour very dear, the "lowness" of the farming is always abused by the English traveller (who thus shows that he knows nothing about either farming or political economy). A farmer, twenty-five years ago, took a very large and fine corn farm: it had been worked on the five-course system, i.e. three white crops in five years; the farmer made a careful calculation whether a four-course husbandry, i.e. two white crops in four years, would not be more profitable; it appeared to come to exactly the same thing. At this juncture a rise of a shilling a week in wages took place; this gave a clear advantage to the four-course, and the farm was at once worked round to the four course shift. In this simple case a small rise in wages brought about a considerable diminution in gross produce, while the loss to the farmer was small. The remarks in this section have been directed to the case, common in the South of England, where there has been within the last twelve years a fall of rent from 25 to 50 per cent. In pasture farms, in rich land, and in potato farms (wherein you can keep one-sixth the land in potatoes), the fall in rent has been much less— sometimes inappreciable.

But, some person may urge, if Government interferes, and compels the farmer to farm higher than he wishes to himself, the gross produce will be more, and the employment for labourers will be at the same time better.

True, and this is the quintessence of Protection. The whole point of Free Trade is to allow capital to be employed where it is most profitable: high farming is only to be preferred (both for individual and nation) to low when it is the more profitable. Capital that cannot be employed to ordinary trade profit on the land must be transferred to other industries where it will earn the ordinary rate of trade profit; or, if there is no trade yielding such profit ready to absorb it in England, the capital must go to the United States or New Zealand and earn an increased profit. As to the labourers, they must follow the capital; or they may starve in England leaving few progeny, while the well-fed labourers of the Western States of America and New Zealand leave large families: this will do instead of emigration.

It is to be noted that great improvements in farming, especially in machinery, have been effected in the last thirty years, largely by the operation of the All England and County Agricultural Societies. I note further that the people who abuse the farmers for bad farming and clamour for Government interference to promote high farming, conspicuously refrain from supporting these agricultural societies.

6. FREE TRADE IN RAILWAYS.

Government might monopolise the retailing of tea in England. At present, in a country town like Exeter or Canterbury, there may be fifty grocers selling tea. In their competition they lay out a good deal in advertisement and handsome shop fronts in the most expensive streets; they keep (the fifty between them) many more hands than are necessary to retail the tea. All this outlay has to come out of the consumer. Government would buy pure tea first-hand in large quantities cheap; a few trustworthy highly-paid officials would test it, value it, and see it done up in sealed packages of sizes from 16 lbs. down to 2 oz.: these might be sold in an odd room attached to the Post Office in each town and village. There can be little doubt but that a saving in capital and labour would thus be effected, while the public would get the tea cheaper and purer than at present. The 2 oz. purchaser, in particular, would pay a good deal less for 2 oz. of real tea than she pays now for 2 oz. of rubbish.

Or,—Government might hand over the tea-retailing of Canterbury and five miles round to a company as a monopoly: the state of things would be something like what we experience in the large stores now: the public would get their tea probably cheaper (quality considered) than at present; the company would make a large profit on their capital. If Government sanctioned two tea-retailing companies at Canterbury, these would probably make a less rate of profit: though, after the first heat of fight was over, they would probably agree to sell the same tea at the same (profitable) rates, and the consumers would gain little out of so restricted a competition. If a new company were to apply for a private Act to enable them to retail tea at Canterbury, the old company would show Parliament that themselves sufficed to satisfy the requirements of the public.

The case of tea is a very specious one. By Government taking to itself each branch of business in succession till all was in Government hands we should arrive at Communism. For each successive interference of Government a reason from economy can generally be found: as in the case of telegraphs, so in the case of tea. The real objection to Government monopolising the retail of tea is, that so long as we live under a system of competition we had better stick to that plan altogether. At every turn of our present struggling system there is waste; but the ultimate effect of competition is to reduce the waste to a minimum. In the extreme case of tea it is pretty clear that the system of stores will, when fully developed, give the public all or nearly all they might hope to get from Government retailing, and at the same time will reduce the loss by competition among tea-retailers.

But there is one industry, one branch of the public service, which should be the very last to be monopolised or restricted by Government, viz., the carrying of passengers and goods from one place to another, especially carrying by railway; and yet this particular industry is hampered by law and restricted by monopolies above all others—as I suppose, most unnecessarily; but I will take a few cases in detail before arguing from the general principle of Free Trade.

There is one railway from London to Brighton: there are two railways from London to Exeter. There are fewer quick trains daily from London to Brighton than from London to Exeter. There are third-class carriages at a penny a mile on all the quick trains from Waterloo to Exeter: from London to Brighton the only penny a mile train starts at an inconvenient hour and travels exceedingly slow. The Brighton charge express fares on every convenient quick train they run; the South-Western have no express fares at all. The South-Western third-class carriages are padded, and as comfortable as the first; the Brighton third-class carriages are bare, very long, and run so badly that the shaking, the rattling of glass, and the draughts, keep everybody (who can possibly afford it) out of them.

Naturally there have been numerous schemes for a second railway from London to Brighton in the course of the last twenty-five years. The present railway company has (they are not to blame for it) opposed each scheme tooth and nail. They have shown that they themselves satisfy the requirements of the public, and at the same time do not make a very high dividend. If a new grocer required an Act of Parliament to set up as a tea-retailer in Canterbury, could not all the existing tea-retailers there prove most triumphantly that an additional grocer was not wanted, and that their own profits were reasonable? It is not too much to say that the greater part of the evidence admitted by Parliamentary Committees against proposed new railways is foolery: without wasting time on it, the Parliamentary Committee might assume as proved that no monopolist trader wants a competitor. But the only safety for the public is in competition. In railway competition the public always profit: if the two companies agree to run at the same fares, the public gain in number and speed of trains, better carriages, and attentive consideration of their comfort. Moreover, in the case of two railways between London and Exeter, or between London and Brighton, the two lines only meet (not then quite) at the two termini; and the public is accommodated at all the new intermediate stations where there was no station at all before.

The North-Western Railway was many years ago opposing a directly competing scheme. They brought before the Parliamentary Committee the late Mr. Horne, whom they justly credited with ability enough to throw dust in the eyes of almost any Parliamentary five. Mr Home's evidence was: "I understand railway traffic as well as anybody; the public are deluded in thinking they would gain by competition: the two companies might fight for a week or two, then they would more wisely agree, and put up their fares above the present North-Western fares, till they had recouped themselves out of the public all they had lost by their fight." This did very well for the Parliamentary Committee; but it is a fallacy. At present the North-Western Railway, though empowered by law to charge three-pence a mile first-class, charge twopence a mile only: why?—because twopence a mile they find to be on the whole the most paying rate. Ergo, after the fight with their directly competing brother was over, they would settle down to twopence a mile again. The public could not lose by the competition; they might gain. All experience shows that they invariably do gain.

In France, Government has restricted the construction of railways very greatly, and protected the monopoly of each existing company closely. The mileage of railway open in France, in proportion to area and population, is very small in comparison with that in England. Moreover, the French lines are worked by quasi-Government officials, whose object is to avoid work, and still more to avoid responsibility, and who will not make the slightest effort to accommodate the public: they do not wish the trade at their station increased. Under this system the traffic on the French railways is low; especially when we consider how little each is interfered with by other lines, and what a broad band of country it has to drain.

The immense progress made by England since 1846, as compared with the progress of France or of Germany, is often attributed *solely* to Free Trade. I believe Free Trade has done much for us: but I am sure that our railway superiority (to France, Germany, etc.) has done much also. Probably no one who has not *resided* some time in a French town (say a station on a main railway 150 miles from Paris as the least favourable case for my argument) can realise the enormous disadvantage by loss of time that a French business man is under, as compared with the Englishman. To get some necessary manufactured article from Paris is a matter of days; during which his machinery may all stand still. The communication with Paris, however, is where the Frenchman suffers least: the number of trains is so small, and the slowness of all (but the express) is such that the "local" traffic is nothing: unless a man intends to go a good many miles he would ride or even walk rather than go by train. He does not mind getting up at 2 a.m. to go to Paris; but he will not get up at that hour to go six or eight miles, especially if he is given no choice as to the hour at which he must return.

But the usual remark about the French railways is, "See how much better they manage these things in France. While our railway companies are all spending their money in fighting and in competition, and pay dividends of 4 or 5 per cent, the French railways have their routes settled by Government engineers, and pay 8 or 10 per cent." I am going to propose a plan for stopping all company fighting in England for ever: but—as to the dividend—it can only mean that, like any other Government monopoly, the French public are being made to pay more for travelling than they need.

As regards the interest of the public, the rate of dividend paid by a great railway company is of very small importance. For many years the South-Western Company paid double the dividend the Great Western did. How did this affect the work each did for the public—the conveyance of passengers and goods? Many common highways have been made by parishes and landowners combined for the public convenience; the capital so laid out paid no direct interest (the road was a highway, not a turnpike): how does this case differ from a railway that pays no dividend on the original stock? If the railway carried me from Exeter to London in five hours for thirteen shillings, what does it matter to me whether the company pays 2-1/2 per cent or 6-1/2 per cent to its original shareholders? In a very few small and special cases we have seen a railway line not pay for the working, and be closed. In a few other cases, where the dividend paid is less than 4-1/2 per cent, it is possible that the utility of the line to the public is less than the loss of the shareholders in a non-paying investment. I say this is a possible and conceivable case—in some very short lines or in some very thinly inhabited districts. Such cases I believe rare. Not rarely the initial cost of the line has been seriously increased by promotion, legal and parliamentary expenses, enormous sums extorted for land, severance, etc.; if these expenses can be done away with, these cases of railways constructed at a loss *on the whole* to the nation may be made fewer still.

The way in which the railway monopoly, the monopoly of the great companies, has grown up is noteworthy. To enable a company to take the land of a private man compulsorily a private Act of Parliament was necessary. The Parliamentary Committees then said, We will not enable you to dispossess forcibly private owners of their land for "a public purpose" unless you further shew that this includes a public advantage. Private owners were of course let in to show cause against a new railway; they always talked like Naboth (the Parliamentary Committees must have been wearied by the continual references to Naboth), but the genuine private owners sold themselves at the last minute; after they had pushed the company up to the highest bid, they well knew that this was above what they could get in the after arbitration, and "closed," withdrawing their opposition the last day in the Committee room. The opposition company, besides the grounds of insufficient need for a new line, etc., always supports and comforts the opposing landowners: but the great resource of the opposing company is to hire a landowner to oppose, especially a local attorney or agent who owns land proposed to be taken by the new line. Such an attorney, employed professionally by the opposing company, cannot be bought off at any price; he is a real Naboth, and in his character of a dispossessed landowner he will fight for the company every point that they cannot decently fight for themselves.

Opposing a railway bill in Parliament has thus become an art; so much so, that no independent small line can be made unless they can get the support of one (at least) of the great companies that are supposed to occupy the area. The lines made (economically often) by the great companies themselves are not primarily designed for the accommodation of the public, but for the private purposes of the great company; sometimes they are made merely to diddle another great company.

It is well to compare the law regarding making a new railway with that for making a new main-drain in the fens. In the latter case the new drain company receives extraordinary powers and may put a rate on the land benefited. In the case of a railway passing through a farm, the common estimate is that it adds a shilling an acre value to the rent of the farm; if there is a station on the farm it often adds much more to the agricultural value. Landlords are up to this: a landlord triumphantly told me, "I got £7000 from that company for cutting me up; but I would have given them £14,000 to cut me up more." (In this case, however, building value came in.) But the disgraceful squabbling of companies, who "sell" any owner without scruple when they come to terms among themselves, has disgusted landlords from actively supporting railway schemes.

A great deal of the opposition between rival companies has been from their point of view an error, as they have subsequently discovered for themselves. When the Great Western Company first opened their station at Basingstoke there was war between them and the South-Western, who thought all their London West-End passengers would transfer themselves to the Great Western at Basingstoke in order to avoid a cab drive from Waterloo to Paddington. Some passengers do so transfer themselves. But *via* Basingstoke a fine trade sprang up between the south of England and the Oxford and Leamington route, which far more than compensated the South-Western Company for the London passengers they lost at Basingstoke. So in a very few years there was peace at Basingstoke, and a through-carriage daily from Birkenhead to Southampton. I think it is impossible to estimate how much one railway company profits by the facilities afforded by all the surrounding companies. The loss at a limited number of competing termini is seen; the gain in the local and cross-country traffic is not.

I propose Free Trade in Railways. I mean that any person or company shall be free to make a railway wherever they please. They will have, before commencing the line, to lodge with the Board of Trade the cost of the land they take as valued in the National Rate Book, with the 30 per cent for compulsory purchase. They will not have to lodge the money where they have come to terms with the owner; and the Board of Trade will allow them to construct the line in reasonable sections. Having lodged their money, the company (or private speculator) will only have to go to work under the (amended) Lands Clauses Consolidation Act.

If this scheme were sanctioned we should have in the course of the next twenty years, *as I estimate*, £100,000,000 additional invested in England profitably—not under Government pressure, but by business men to get interest. Even where the new lines paid little interest we should get the accommodation of the public. We should have no big village without its railway; and we should have a great extension of private sidings. On the eastern half of England we might get a great number of narrow gauge steam trams running along the present trunk roads. (Suppose a steam tram from London to York by the Royston route, going through all the towns, running trams an hour apart all day, going eight miles an hour through the towns, sixteen or twenty miles an hour in the country, taking up and setting down everywhere, would it not pay?)

The only objection to Free Trade in railways is that it would injure the existing railway monopoly. Under this principle no monopoly ever would have been or ever will be put down. But I believe the existing great companies would very generally gain by Free Trade in railways.

For, first, few new railways would be in direct competition with the old. The old lines have level roads; they can run quicker and with less wear and tear than the new ones, which would generally have steeper gradients. The new Free Trade lines would be in the main a network in the interstices of the present lines. By this the existing companies would gain enormously; they would be the trunk lines which the network would feed. It is true that there would soon be a second line to Brighton; the present Brighton Company would possibly pay as good a dividend then as they do now. But if they did not, it would only show how they tax the public now as well as hinder trade. I am not bound to show that the monopolists would profit by Free Trade; I deny that the monopolists have any vested interest in their monopoly, or that Parliament, i.e. the nation, has made any covenant with them that their monopoly shall never be invaded.

I have suggested three great changes: (1) Perfect Free Trade at all our ports; (2) The exploitation of the land through the National Rate Book machinery; (3) Free Trade in Railways. Of these the last is clearly advisable, nor is there anything (in my opinion) to be urged on the other side. At the same time it is not less important than either of the two other suggestions. But the three would work best together—each aiding and reacting on the other; they would thus provide "progress" (which means comfort to all classes) in England for at least two generations of men. If there was no National Rate Book, the new railways would have to pay exorbitantly for the land they took up under the existing arbitration system; they would be relieved merely from the parliamentary opposition of other companies and of private individuals. The private owner must be deprived of his present privilege of parliamentary opposition, which gives him the power to extort an exorbitant price for his land—because a company can always oppose in the garb of some private owner whom they have hired.

A less but important branch of this reform is the narrowing of Government interference under pretence of protecting the public. Great expenses are thus thrown on railway companies. The companies cannot, therefore, charge increased fares, but such expenses diminish the number of new railway schemes brought forward. Nor do Government rules protect the public so well as the old plan (abolished by Chief-Justice Cockburn) of making the railway company pay for killing or injuring people. Now, after a great railway smash, the company comes forward and shows that there was no negligence on their part; that in the signals, breaks, etc., they had satisfied all the Board of Trade regulations, and the injured passengers can get nothing. The real way to protect the passengers is to allow the company to make their own arrangements, and to compel them to pay heavily for killing and maiming passengers. This is quite defensible in theory, as in the case of manslaughter by an individual we give him some punishment out of our civilised respect for human life, though he may have been little to blame. Great cost is thrown on railway companies (i.e. much injury is done the public) by standing orders (cast-iron orders) about gradients, etc. The company's solicitors order the company's engineer to comply with standing orders at all costs rather than introduce any special clause. The consequence is that we see much money spent and a most inconvenient level-crossing placed at the entrance to some large town, where a steep gradient for two hundred yards on a straight piece of road (to which there is no objection) would have avoided all difficulty. The responsibility in all such cases should be thrown on the company, and Government interference abolished.

7. REFORM IN LAND LAW.

The transfer of stock in the name of two trustees in the funds is done in a few minutes at small expense. The transfer of land in South Australia is done in a few minutes at small expense at the Government registry. The transfer of land in England requires an uncertain time and cost—usually some weeks, and 5 per cent on the purchase money; sometimes months, and 10 to 25 per cent on the purchase money. It is equally expensive and slow in the register counties of York and Middlesex. The Acts of Brougham, Bethell, Cairns, to facilitate transfer have not materially reduced the evil. In many cases, however much the land may be wanted for public or other purposes, the lawyers tell you that no title can be made without a private Act of Parliament—so effectually has the land been tied up.

The common idea is that this peculiar difficulty, delay, and cost in the transfer of land arise from the law of inheritance and the legal machinery of entail; but stock in the funds can be virtually entailed and made to "follow the estate," and yet this stock can be transferred just as readily as any other stock.

The explanation is known to every lawyer; but I have met with more than one Member of Parliament who, though blatant about entail, understood no more about the matter than a chimney-sweep.

The point is that, under English law, the trusts in the case of stock attach to the trustees, not to the stock; in the case of land, the trusts attach to the land itself as well as to the trustees. Hence, when I purchase stock of trustees I need not trouble about how they apply the purchase money; in the case of land I have to go into the whole title.

A simple illustration. I provide for a daughter £300 a year by putting £10,000 in the hands of two trustees in the funds. Should the trustees prove rascals, sell the stock, and decamp with the money, my daughter will lose everything; the purchaser from the trustees can hold the stock clear of all charges or liability. But if I provide for my daughter by charging an estate with £300 a year for her, then however wrongfully that estate may be sold, mortgaged, or otherwise dealt with, she gets safely her £300 a year. If the bank B has advanced money on mortgage on that estate, not knowing the existence of the charge of £300 a year for my daughter's benefit, the law simply says to the bank, "It was your business to know; you should have completely investigated the title before you advanced your money."

It follows, therefore, that if, with a Government Land Registry Office (say one for each county), you required the purchaser only to get in the legal estate, *i.e.* holding him not responsible for the trusts or the application of the purchase money, then land could be transferred exactly as money in the funds is now, in spite of all the complications of our law (or rather custom) of entail.

The law of entail in England (so called) is not what the popular orators suppose. The eldest son inherits really; that is, if there be no will, no settlement, or other disposition of the property. But there nearly always is. It is a very rare thing for the heir-at-law to take land (except some very small pieces) by the law of inheritance. As to entail, it is practically carried out by a continued system of surrender and re-settlement—a device of lawyers which is, in its historical development, an evasion (rather than a part) of the law. Nevertheless, I think it is a matter of importance that the shackles which fetter land should be loosened, and that the present powers of owners to tie up land legally should be very much curtailed. It is a sad proof of the way riches cling to the heart of man even when he is leaving this world, that, whatever powers of tying up land are sanctioned, an owner will usually exert them to the uttermost. He is leaving his property, but he will keep a hold on it fifty years after he is dead if he can. He will, after exhausting his powers in life interests, leave the residuum to an unborn child "in strict tail-male so far as the rules of law will permit;" and he will stick in a springing use to effect that, if his greatnephew, the Rev. George, should ever from an Anglican become a pervert to Roman Catholicism, he shall take no benefit under the will.

Now the fact is that all tying up is to the detriment of the public. No man can provide for all contingencies. Indeed he can see so little a way ahead that in a few years it frequently happens that all the careful provisions of the will are working exactly as the testator would have desired them not to work. Land tied up is always worth less to the owner because it is tied up; and we have seen that the interest of the commonwealth is the sum of the interests of all its component members. When you tell me that an estate is now of small value to its life-owner and unget-at-able for any public purposes, in consequence of a will made by a man who died twenty years ago, it appears to me that you shew me convincingly that we have not Free Trade in land.

I would propose that, either by will, settlement, or other instrument, an owner should be able to give any number of life interests, and nothing more; all trusts being placed outside the law. The first objection will be that if the powers of owners are so restricted, the desire for the ownership of land will be lessened: the value of all the land in England will fall. This might be so, I admit, to some extent; and it would favour the employ of the land for agricultural profit.

The next objection is that it would become necessary to give land (and money) directly to women without the intervention of trustees: that women do not understand business and require to be taken care of. My reply is that they always will require to be taken care of unless they are entrusted with the management of their own affairs. The loss to the nation, the expenses, the sacrifice of time and labour in trusteeships, have now assumed gigantic proportions. If women were given their own property to manage, some would (at first) fool it away: we know what high interest, adventurers, unprincipled persons, etc., can effect. But each woman defrauded or stripped of her property to starve would be a warning to all the rest: in a few years women would manage their property just as well as men. I believe they would manage it better. A smaller percentage of women would gamble on the Stock Exchange, the Mining Exchange, Austrian and Spanish lotteries, and horse-races; and a much smaller percentage of women would embark in desperate "business" speculations, heavy purchases of foreign produce, etc.

It should be noted that in cutting down the powers of owners to legally tie up, I do not interfere with honourable trusteeships of any kind not enforceable by law or in equity. Such exist now, and more largely than is generally supposed. The absolute devises and bequests to friends (not relatives) are often on private (not expressed) trust to provide for illegitimate children or numerous other purposes which a man may not wish to parade to his family.

8. EQUALISING OF TAXATION.

There has been no readjustment of the land tax for very many years. It is a property rate, and originally was rateably levied at four shillings in the pound. By the small increase in value of some land, the large increase in value of other land, since the days of Queen Anne, it has now become unequal in the highest degree. The farm A, gross rental £100 a year, has a land tax of £5 a year; the suburban estate B, gross rental £1000 a year, has a land tax of £2:10s. a year. The land tax assessors were sworn in annually (twenty years ago, and may be still) to assess the tax equally, but it was perfectly understood that the tax was to be collected every year on the old long-standing assessment.

Suppose that the estates A and B above were reassessed, and that the land tax on A was put 15s. per annum, that on B £6:15s. a year. Land tax can be redeemed at about thirty years' purchase. The effect of the readjustment would have been to take about £120 from the owner of B and give it in a lump sum to the owner of A. It is probable that the present owners of both A and B (or predecessors under whom they claim) had purchased the estates A and B after the land tax had become fixed on them, and the amount of land tax would then have been fully considered in the price paid.

We see thus that in the case of the land tax, as we saw above of the tithe, and as is also the case in any tax permanently on, a disturbance of the existing taxation is inequitable. This point is so much misunderstood that I will give one more illustration.

I am purchasing an estate, intending to farm it myself. There are 400 acres of land, and I reckon the land worth 30s. an acre. I am willing to give twenty-five years' purchase. I find the tithe is £100 a year. I therefore propose to give twenty-five times £500 = £12,500 for the land. But before the bargain is completed I find that the tithe is £150 a year. I at once sink my bid to twenty-five times £450 = £11,250, and buy the estate at that price. The next year some financier "equalises" the tithe, and my tithe is reduced to £100. Is it not clear that, by the equalisation, I pocket £1250, and somebody else loses it?

New taxes when imposed should be "equal," as far as can be arranged. When a legacy duty was imposed, it would have been just to impose a succession duty also. But, after the legacy duty had been imposed twenty years with no succession duty, it was similarly inequitable to put on a succession duty; for quantities of land had been bought in the interval of twenty years at a slightly higher price than if there had been no legacy duty, because there was no succession duty.

The proposal for "equalising" taxes is usually put forward in order to get a somewhat larger gross income from the taxes equalised, or as a political cry. Nothing can be more absurd than the cry that the land is over-burdened in comparison with other property. There is no comparison in the case. Some land being tithe free, some land tax free, some nearly rate free, those persons who do not trouble themselves to master the political economy may yet be satisfied that the "burdens" of the land affect neither the farmer, the labourer, nor the produce of the farm; the burdens fall *wholly* on the landlord (a farmer with a lease being, as above shown, a part landlord). The efforts of some Conservative orators for the last twenty-five years to prove the contrary are erroneous in the reasoning; or I should say, much of the "reasoning" does not hang together at all. Without formally refuting these efforts, I repeat that they are fully refuted in the result.

It is therefore that I have insisted above that, in order to carry out the proposed ransom of the land, a new Property Rate, separate from and in addition to all other taxes, is necessary. Though the manner of levying a National Property Rate which I have proposed lends itself very nicely to getting in such an extra tax, it is not at all on that ground that I have suggested the new manner of levy. The object of the new manner of levy and the sycophants is to get every piece of land in the country into the hands of that man who can make most of it; including herein as an important item the cheap and easy acquisition of land required for Government, public and commercial (railway, etc.) enterprises.

In any great reform of our whole system of taxation a disturbance of existing interests must take place. Though I would not disturb existing interests for the sake of mere equalisation or official beauty of work, I would not let the fear of disturbing private interests stand in the way of any real or important reform. The introduction of Universal Free Trade and the abolition of all duties would be accompanied by a disturbance; but, as far as I can see, no one would lose, while many would gain enormously.

On the same ground of equality of new taxation I should propose to replace the amount now levied in duties mainly by an income tax. That is a perfectly level tax; the idea that temporary incomes ought to pay a lower rate is fallacious. We are all agreed to tax the poor at a *lower* rate; we have now a section of advanced Radicals proposing to tax the rich at a higher rate. One present candidate for Parliament is even willing to tax people of £100,000 a year and upwards at nineteen shillings in the pound. This of course, or anything approaching it, is unpractical. But I have suggested above, as a rough plan in accordance with the existing one, eight-pence a week on incomes of £1 a week, twelvepence a week on incomes of £2 a week, sixteen-pence a week on incomes of £3 a week and upwards. The question may very fairly be raised, Why stop this process at £3? why not continue the series and develop it into a mathematical law? This might be done more easily with a sixpenny income tax than a heavy one. To tax earnings and savings (that is an income tax) instead of expenditure can only be carried a certain way; if the tax is large enough to diminish saving and promote living up to one's income, and at the same time to send capital abroad, its effects would be serious. For a particular and noble purpose I have suggested sixteen-pence in the pound (which we bore without serious inconvenience in the Russian war); I should imagine twenty to twenty-four pence in the pound about the maximum that could be imposed for any purpose—such as the prevention of hostile invasion. It must be noted that more than the maximum bearable cannot be put on large incomes, £100,000 a year, etc., any more than on small ones. Indeed it is rather the contrary; for persons with large incomes are usually the very people who already invest largely abroad, and who could (and would) transfer their capital rapidly out of the country if they were subjected to anything like confiscation.

Instead therefore of proceeding *upwards* in our income tax sliding-scale we must proceed downwards. Taking sixteen-pence in the pound as the maximum rate we can impose on the big fish, the problem will be, What is the highest income to which you will allow any remission from the maximum rate? I think those having above £150 a year possess more than the necessaries for healthful existence; looking therefore to the equity and productiveness of the tax, I suggested remission to those earning less than £3 a week.

9. WEALTH OF THE NATION.

The Wealth of Nations is a well-considered title. The economists anterior to Adam Smith conceived England as surrounded by a barrier impassable to property and money except by trade. In trade there was an exchange apparently on equal terms; but the old economists saw a difference in nature between imports and exports; when wool was sold to Flanders gold was received, and remained somewhere in the nation; it formed the national purchasing power, and could hire mercenaries or otherwise command foreign labour and productions. Inversely, when we imported wine or tea, we had to part with a portion of our national purchasing power, while the wine and tea went down our throats, leaving nothing in its place. It appeared clear that for any increase in national wealth the value of the exports must exceed that of the imports. Every well-prepared boy can now show in ten minutes' scribbling in a Government examination the ridiculous folly of the old economists; but several of them were experienced London merchants, and perhaps were not the complete idiots they are now triumphantly shown to be. If they had been asked whether wool was a part of the national wealth they might have returned an answer that their modern detractors are not quite prepared for.

Adam Smith and his followers, and still more closely Ricardo, divided their Political Economy into two parts: in the first they consider the wealth of the nation without the "complication" of foreign trade, *i.e.* they, in fact, contemplate no money or goods as going out or coming in whatever. They then in separate chapters, forming a big appendix, consider the effects of Foreign Trade as a series of exchanges. They do not discuss even the payment of a lump sum of gold to a victorious nation. Senior, in his *Handbook of Political Economy*, has considered, first, the economy of the world conceived as a solitary, island of small size in a world-covered sea; secondly, he treats foreign trade by conceiving two such islands. There is no better way of treating Political Economy than this; and it is well for the beginner to conceive the solitary island with fifty (or a limited number of) families only on it, and work through the ordinary theorems (with figures) in this restricted case. Whatever is true of the fifty families in a small island must be true for 5,000,000 families in a big island.

The facilities of modern communications have caused most countries to differ in their circumstances materially from the conditions assumed by Adam Smith and his successors as axioms. In the case of England, owing to its numerous wealthy colonies, gigantic foreign trade, and consequently world-over-spread capital, the circumstances are so completely altered that many results of the grammar of Political Economy no longer apply even in the rough to England. If Adam Smith had been asked what would happen to England if the imports for one year exceeded the exports by £150,000,000 sterling, he would have given the same answer as his predecessors, who reckoned wealth in gold and silver, or more probably he would have declined answer, pronouncing such a state of things an impossible conception. It is now as difficult to treat politico-economically the wealth of the nation as the wealth of Warwickshire—a difficulty that Adam Smith would have shrunk from.

It is true that every abstract proposition concerning rent, capital, and wages now (and always) holds true for the whole world; but, so conceived, the propositions give no practical result. These things do not lesson the value of the science of Political Economy, Mr. Ranken or Dr. Pole would estimate very highly the value of a knowledge of elementary mechanics to the humblest engineer, though such elementary mechanics might not extend to the consideration of friction, etc., and might not be applicable to any bridge or steam-engine.

Of this £150,000,000 that is now annually remitted to England, not in the way of exchange, some small portion is transferred by wealthy Australians returning to settle in England for purchase of houses, etc., in England; but by far the greater portion is the interest of capital owned by men resident in England, but invested abroad: it may be shortly termed tribute. This is mainly invested in the Colonies and India; New Zealand and Australia taking large shares. There is also much English capital invested in Continental railways, etc.; but it is noteworthy how capital (as well as commerce) follows the flag. The English capital invested in the United States is absolutely large, but relatively (to that invested in Canada, etc.) very small. It is certain that if the United States were under Queen Victoria the amount of English capital invested there would be far greater than at present.

As far as England is concerned this £150,000,000 a year is a tribute paid her by the rest of the world. New Zealand or South Australia may take up a million sterling in London (because they get the loan placed there at 5 or 6 per cent, while the local rate of interest in Australia is far higher) in order to make a railway which perhaps pays the local Government as much as the interest of the money they give to England. Still, the capital being once fixed in Australia while (by hypothesis) the stock is held in England, the result is equivalent to a tribute.

All Liberal stump-orators now agree in telling the agricultural population that their improved position is due to Free Trade (in wheat), and that therefore they should vote for the Liberals. Nothing is done more confidently in politics and history than the settling the causes of events, or predicting what would have been the course of events had some result been different, as, for instance, had the separation of the United States from England not occurred. The truth is that in politics causes are many; they act and react on each other in their operations; and to say exactly how much is due to one cause, or how much that cause acting alone would have effected, is impossible. To get some judgment how much of the present prosperity of the agricultural labourers (admitted on all sides as compared with their position in 1846) is due to free importation of wheat alone, let us (merely as a scientific artifice) imagine that a regular sliding-scale duty on wheat were put on now, bringing wheat to 48s. a quarter permanently. What would be the effect on the agricultural population? We may suppose that the produce of the duty, were it five or eight millions, or any other sum, was employed in remitting the duties on tea or other productions generally consumed by agricultural labourers. The placing of wheat at 48s. a quarter permanently would at once recall a good deal of capital to the land, it would carry out further the margin of cultivation, and at the same time cause a higher farming of that within the non-existing margin; in both ways it would raise the demand for agricultural labour, and would raise wages.

On the whole, I incline to think that a sliding-scale duty on wheat up to 48s. a quarter would not perceptibly alter the position of the agricultural labourer, or might possibly improve it: it would lower the wages and diminish the profits of capital in other trades. This is not (as before explained) a fair way of arguing the question; because it is impossible to calculate the indirect effects of Free Trade in wheat, which ultimately came round to benefit the agricultural labourer.

But considering how the efficiency of the agricultural labourer has been improved by improved machines since 1846, it is hardly possible to doubt that the agricultural labourer is much more indebted to the engineers than to the Corn Law League for his improved position. Under "machines" too may be included railway communications: also let us not forget how much the agricultural labourer owes, not only to drills and mowing-machines, but to boot-sewing machines, improved tea-ships, etc.

If we look to the general increase of wealth in England since 1846, the first thing that strikes us is the increase in the tribute, which is about thrice what it was. This increase is largely imperial, i.e. due to colonisation, annexation, etc. But here again we must not overlook the reaction of causes on each other: our Free Trade in corn, our improvements in machinery and ships, have so largely contributed to spread our empire that it becomes impossible to disentangle the separate work, or indeed to speak of any one cause as a simple element: the causes all act together.

England is the most comfortable country in the world for a rich man to live in, and consequently rich men congregate there; or, if they travel, keep a headquarters there. In this way we have congregated a disproportionate population in England. It may be argued that it would be a healthier economic state if the exports and imports balanced, and if the population of England was no larger than the country itself could grow wheat for, *at a price not exceeding 40s. a quarter*. However that may be, the important point for the working men of England to mark is, that every loss of rich men resident, every loss of tribute, every reduction of the wage-fund, every pressure on the population to emigrate, everything that leads in the direction of a self-supporting England, means immediate pressure on the poor, with reduction of wages. That is the only way emigration could be by natural law enforced. It is the poor, the labouring population, who are so hugely interested in the empire. Of all the follies taught to the labouring man the most foolish is the doctrine that the empire abroad is maintained to provide incomes for the rich, at the cost of the taxes paid for wars by the poor. It matters comparatively little to the rich whether they live at Florence or Dresden four or eight months in the year, whether the population of England is to be maintained stationary, to increase at its present rate of increase, or to be squeezed down to half its present number: but it matters vitally to the poor. Whether, ultimately, after our empire is gone and the population of England is stationary at fifteen millions say, the poor in England would be better off than now is a very difficult question, concerning which doctors differ; but it is absolutely certain that during the Banting process, in the reduction of the population down to that fifteen millions by a process of starvation and emigration, continued for two generations of men, the poor would have to go through experiences altogether novel. It is a thing that would revolutionise England; and in spite of the superior education of our labourers might lead to a break up of society. Starvation and bankruptcy make any and every man a Radical if not a Communist.

To keep the poor comfortable for the present and for many years immediately in front of us, we require a continual increase in the wealth laid out in England annually in the purchase of labour. The growth of the empire, the profitable investment of capital in foreign countries (whereof the interest is paid and consumed in England), is one great resource: the profitable investment of capital in England itself is the other great, probably safer, resource. To effect this we require every acre of land to fall into the hand of the man (or company) who can make most of it: we require a Universal Free Trade that shall render our hold on the commerce of the world secure until all nations adopt Universal Free Trade (when we shall gain so much in other ways that we shall be able to afford to share our monopoly with others); we require the removal of all restraints on railways, tramways, electric lights, etc., that hamper or prevent the employment of capital in England (in other words, that send English capital abroad). Finally, underlying the whole, and as the prime cause that shall induce capitalists to employ their capital in England rather than to send it abroad, we require the labour of every working man to be in the highest degree efficient: this retards the fall of the natural rate of profits to a minimum, and the attainment of the stationary state. Whatever ideal beauty has been discovered in the stationary state by J. S. Mill, it is pretty clear that England is not approaching it. It is as difficult for us to stand still as it is impossible to go back; and our only (third) course open (for the present and for many years to come) is to progress.